Michael Jordan

Michael Jordan

— The Amazing —
Six-Time NBA Champion

Jack Clary

ACKNOWLEDGEMENTS

The author wishes to acknowledge the invaluable
assistance that was provided by the Chicago Bulls public
relations department, and by Rick Brewer, the sports
information director at the University of North Carolina.

The author also utilized a variety of published sources,
including *Sports Illustrated*, *The Sporting News*, the
Boston Globe, the *Chicago Tribune*, the *Chicago
Tribune*, the *Chicago Sun-Times*, and the *Raleigh* (N.C.)
News & Observer.

Also, grateful thanks go to my editor, Jean Martin, of
Brompton Books, as well as the designer, Don
Longabucco; the picture editor, Kathy Schneider; and
the indexer, Elizabeth A. McCarthy.

Jack Clary
Stow, Massachusetts

Previous pages: *Whether
he's dressed to kill* (page 1)
or dressed to thrill (page
2), *Michael Jordan is one
of the most recognizable
athletes in the world.*

These pages: *Michael
Jordan soars and swoops
to the basket with his
distinctive style –
including his protruding
tongue – that often has
caused his own
teammates and the
opposition to stop playing
and watch in awe.*

CONTENTS

INTRODUCTION

Michael Jordan is the most exciting basketball player in the game's history.

His unique style of shooting, passing and rebounding has brought the sport an entirely new dimension of soaring, flying, leaping and graceful swoops over the hardwood that have excited millions in every age group. He has so captivated the game's fans, ardent and casual alike, that his scoring totals in a given game really are secondary to the show he puts on.

Two decades ago, Julius Erving, the famed Dr. J., lit up the scene with his flying dunks, but Jordan has taken that particular art form of basketball ballet quantum leaps forward because he can do it from any part of the court – going end-to-end, half court or from a standing stop under the basket.

Jordan is a complete player, and while he lights up a nation with his offensive talent, he puts as much effort – and care – into playing defense. He has said on many occasions that he prefers defense to offense, and takes greater pride in doing a complete defensive job in a game than in scoring 30 or 40 points.

While he led the Chicago Bulls to their first NBA

Opposite: *Jordan's amazing athletic skills allow him to do unbelievable things with his body, such as seeming to stop in mid-air before launching an underhanded scoop shot from the middle of the key.*

Right: *Jordan often has been compared to one of his boyhood idols, former NBA star Julius Erving, the famed Dr. J., because of his great flair as he drives to the basket and stuffs home his shots.*

championship in 1991, Jordan had been a bright star on the basketball scene since his freshman year at the University of North Carolina when his basket, with 15 seconds to play, gave the Tar Heels the NCAA championship in a one-point victory over heavily-favored Georgetown. For two years after that, he was the nation's most celebrated player, a two-time All-America and chosen "College Player of the Year" by many publications. This made Michael Jordan a marked man – marked by the game's aficionados for future stardom, and by

opponents as the one man they had to stop.

Jordan has fought and won his battles on the basketball court in his own flamboyant style, and he has mastered the added burdens of fame and fortune with both grace and savvy. He left the game in 1993 after leading the Bulls to three straight NBA titles to pursue a baseball career, and returned two years later to lead Chicago to another three titles. He is unquestionably the greatest player in the sport's history while becoming the world's most popular athlete during the 1990s.

Opposite: *Jordan's game-winning shot with 5.8 seconds to play in the sixth game of the 1998 Finals gave the Bulls and Jordan their second "three-peat" in eight years.*

Right: *Jordan pauses during filming of his "Air Jordan" Nike commercial. He became the highest paid professional athlete ever in 1997 when he signed a one-year contract for $30.6 million. It has been estimated that Jordan's talent produced $10 billion worth of world-wide economic activity during his time in the NBA.*

Below: *Michael enjoys the fruits of his labor in his red Ferarri Testarossa.*

PART I
TAR HEEL BLUE AND OLYMPIC GOLD

Considering how Michael Jordan has so dominated the basketball world for most of the past decade, it is hard to imagine that he was once thought to be just another kid who loved to play basketball and who, even in his own young mind at the time, felt he would be fortunate to play in a Division II school before forever fading from the sport.

Those who believed that really didn't know Michael Jordan, nor did Michael really know himself at the time. They also hadn't factored in all of the elements which go into making a basketball star: Mother Nature, hard work, God-given skill, more hard work, and a bit of luck.

Jordan is today the sport's most visible star, a multi-millionaire and the most prosperous player in the game's history. But when he was growing up in the seacoast town of Wilmington, North Carolina, in the 1960s and 1970s, his life was a far cry from the riches and adulation that he now enjoys.

His parents, James and Delores Jordan, were great success stories in their own right. They were the offspring of eastern North Carolina sharecroppers who set out to build a better life for the five children they were raising, and they did it the old-fashioned way — by hard work. James Jordan was hired as a mechanic at General Electric's plant in Wilmington in 1967, and

Opposite: *Jordan was a sensation from the very beginning of his career, at the University of North Carolina. He was selected to the All-America team in both his sophomore and junior seasons, and was picked by* The Sporting News *as Player of the Year in both of those seasons.*

Right: *Jordan admits that the influence of his parents, James and Delores, was the most important factor in helping him to achieve stardom. From them, he honed his renowned work ethic and inherited the competitiveness that had helped them to succeed in their lives. James Jordan's tragic death in 1993 was a great shock to his family and to all who knew what a special relationship Michael had had with his dad.*

worked his way through jobs as a dispatcher and fore-man to become supervisor of the spare parts depart-ment.

From his dad, Jordan has said, he inherited his admirable work ethic, extroverted personality, sense of humor, and great patience — the latter to be of special importance because, as his star began to rise, so too did the demands from outside sources for all of his spare time. Those who are close to him say that they never have seen a star of such dimension so will-ing to do all that is required to satisfy people wanting his time for pictures, autographs, interviews and a myriad of other demands that mark the life of a super-star.

Delores Jordan is responsible for the competitive side of Michael's personality, which she exhibited in her own right by starting her career as a bank teller at a branch office in Wilmington, and then becoming head of customer relations at the main office.

Michael's potential for hard work and perseverance came from his home environment, and from a firm guiding hand from his parents that steered him in the correct direction during his younger years.

Not unlike any young kid who loves to spend his spare time playing basketball, he found it more pleasurable to forego some of his classes in favor of playing the game in the school gym. Three times during his freshman year at Laney High School in Wil-mington, he was suspended for cutting classes. After

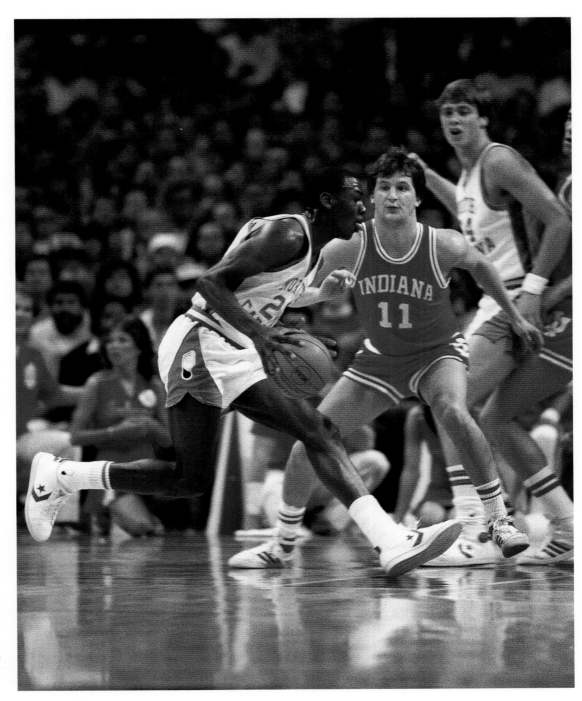

Opposite left: Jordan salutes his mother Delores, who was a sharecropper's daughter and worked to become a bank executive in Wilmington, North Carolina.

Opposite right: At Laney High School in Wilmington, Jordan was a non-descript player until his final two seasons. At one time, he believed that his career would go no further than the small college level, until his coach contacted North Carolina coach Dean Smith.

Right: Jordan became only the fourth freshman ever to start for Dean Smith at North Carolina. He had impressed his future coach at a basketball camp while convincing himself that he could play at the major college level, though his first choice at the time was the Tar Heels' big rival, North Carolina State.

the third infraction, James Jordan sat his son down and asked him, "What do you want to do with your life?"

"I want to go to college and play basketball," Michael replied.

Fair enough, his father thought, but first he must get through high school. He knew that his son needed a strong dose of discipline to keep him attending classes and to allow his love of basketball to be fulfilled only when the school day ended.

"I had two directions to go," his father said. "I could have let things ride and hope he'd grow out of it, or I could make my point right away and get him straightened out before it was too late."

James Jordan took the second option. Like most fathers would, he told his son the only way to get into college was by working hard in the classroom. He offered his son a choice: do it my way and succeed, or do it your way and fall short.

"My father talking to me really made me think," Jordan has said. "I knew he was right and I tried to change. I concentrated more on my schoolwork because I set a goal to excel in the classroom to reach college and I had to work to reach it."

Jordan always appreciated his dad's role, and his dad was always his biggest fan. His father saw all but one of his games at North Carolina, and Michael said that he never relaxed during pre-game warmups until he spotted him. And, until his tragic death in 1993, James Jordan was always a part of Michael's great moments in the NBA.

Mother Nature then did her part. Michael was just an ordinary kid, a skinny six-foot, one-inch sophomore who was only good enough to play on Laney High's junior varsity. But within a year, he grew another five inches, and after his senior season, he was good enough to compete against college players in the U.S. Olympic Committee's National Sports Festival.

Jordan's own college future had been settled, thanks to Mike Brown, Laney's athletic director and a North Carolina alumnus, who had called UNC basketball coach Dean Smith. "We might have a player for you down here," Brown told Smith, without knowing that Jordan really favored North Carolina State, one of the Tar Heels' arch rivals, because his idol at the time was the Wolfpack's All-American, David Thompson. Jordan had begun to pattern some of his game after Thompson, who had gained great renown for his leaping and jumping ability.

All it took to convince Jordan was one summer at Smith's basketball camp at Chapel Hill, and Jordan signed his letter of intent to become a Tar Heel. Yet, there was also doubt in his own mind whether he could play at the Atlantic Coast Conference level until his first pickup game at the school, when he played against established Tar Heel players Al Wood, Mitch Kupchak and James Worthy (the latter two would go on to be members of the world champion Los Angeles Lakers during the 1980s.) The game had attracted quite a crowd, and Jordan recalls being very nervous and insecure, as any 18-year-old might be having just come from high school to play with established college stars. Wood was guarding him in a situation where the next basket would win the game, and he took Wood to the baseline when seven-foot Geoff Crompton came over to help out on defense. Thinking he was trapped, Jordan leaped toward the basket, and, as he

recalls, "I just kept going up, and I went over both of them and dunked the ball."

At first, he couldn't believe what he had just accomplished, but it was also the last time he ever felt insecure in college basketball. He brought his determination for personal improvement and his competitiveness to the team, as well as an ability to play within coach Dean Smith's very demanding team concept, where there were to be no great stars, but only players willing to blend their talents for the overall good of the team. In retrospect, Smith's concept is hard to imagine, considering that such future NBA greats as Worthy, Sam Perkins and Brad Dougherty were among Jordan's teammates.

To perfect his skills, Jordan played basketball nearly every day, and he was renowned for his hard work at practice. No one can recall Smith ever having to get after him in a practice session, rather remarkable because a college basketball season is long and can be fraught with distractions from school, social activities and the campus environment.

The mental discipline that Jordan's father had in-

Opposite top: *Dean Smith, the most successful basketball coach in North Carolina history, is renowned for his very controlled style of play that helped Jordan perfect every facet of his game.*

Opposite bottom: *One of Jordan's teammates during his freshman year was future Lakers star James Worthy (left), while Tar Heels teammate Sam Perkins (right) was selected just after Jordan in the 1984 NBA draft by the Dallas Mavericks.*

Right: *Jordan, shown here shooting against coach Bobby Knight's Indiana Hoosiers, led the Tar Heels to the 1983 Holiday Festival title at New York's Madison Square Garden, but he didn't even make the all-tournament team because he played so well under Smith's controlled system.*

Opposite: After Jordan won Atlantic Coast Conference Freshman of the Year honors, Coach Dean Smith sent him home with instructions to work on his defense. The result: Smith allowed Jordan to freelance on defense and go after the ball whenever he believed he had a chance to make an impact.

Right: Jordan had a fine shooting year as a freshman, as displayed here in the NCAA championships, but thanks to a fan's letter during his sophomore season pointing out that the arc on his field goals was lower than on his free throws, he soon improved his shooting style.

stilled in him as a young teenager paid off throughout his college career. After he had canned the winning basket in the 1982 NCAA title game — an amazing climax to any season, but for a freshman, an unbelievable one — Smith sent him home with orders to work on his defense.

The next season, he won Smith's post-game award for the best defensive performance 12 times; he hadn't won it at all as a freshman. Smith termed his defensive play "three times better than as a freshman," and made an exception to his own rule for only the third time ever in his coaching career at North Carolina by allowing Jordan to go for the ball whenever he thought he had an opportunity to make a play. He stole the ball 78 times that season.

After his sophomore season, in which he was selected for the All-America team, Smith sent him home with instructions to improve his ball-handling skills. He became a superb ball-handler, a skill that has since made him one of the NBA's best guards. Jordan didn't stop there: he had noticed from film study after his sophomore season — and from fan mail sent by some incisive observers — that his jump shot arched higher than his free throw. He worked on putting less rainbow into the shot, and for the first time, he won the week-long, pre-season shooting competition.

"I never saw a guy as talented as Michael work as hard," teammate Matt Doherty observed that year. "His work ethic is intense, demanding, all business.

He really doesn't need to work on anything. Maybe Coach is just keeping him humble."

Excessive pride was never a problem with Jordan, because he was never satisfied with his game. His competitiveness was legendary at North Carolina, and has carried over to his pro game. Losing at anything makes him absolutely miserable. At North Carolina, when he played cards or his favorite game, Monopoly, he wouldn't quit until he was ahead — even if it meant playing until dawn. Such instances were the only times that a darker side of his nature showed, and he freely admits he has been embarrassed by some of his antics after such innocent competitions.

"It's an instinct that makes me love to win and hate to lose at any game," he has said. "My older brother Larry used to beat me in one-on-one basketball games. He'd say something about it and I'd get ticked off and fight him."

But it also is a quality that has driven him to greatness, enabling him to come up with impossible plays when a game is on the line. "When it comes down close to the end, I just get kind of inspired and give that extra 10 percent,' he has said.

That doesn't mean that either his Tar Heel or his Bulls teammates have automatically looked to him to win a game. "I just think they look for someone to create something and I just try to do that," he said. "I

penetrate, pass off, and maybe set a pick or grab an offensive rebound — anything I can do to spark the team."

He showed that mentality during his junior year, when the Tar Heels easily won the Holiday Festival tournament at Madison Square Garden in New York City with typical balanced scoring and Jordan didn't even make the all-tournament team. But all of his work at North Carolina produced a player able to shoot from 20 feet from the basket; to play the post-up game near the basket; and to jump over, or drive around, defenders to complete an unending array of spectacular dunk shots.

"I don't know what I'm going to do when I start those plays," he has said. "Really, I just want the two points and I'm going for the high percentage shot, which for me is a dunk. I just want to make it, regardless of how I do it. It gets me excited, and it gets everyone on the team excited. We seem to just start playing basketball after one of those."

Jordan's play at North Carolina got everyone excited, and one of the most amazing achievements of his three-year varsity career was his ability to handle all of the media attention. He wisely heeded Coach Smith's suggestion to take a radio-TV course so he could better understand how the media worked, and then followed Smith's advice on learning what *not* to say. Rick Brewer, the school's sports information

Opposite: *Jordan was never considered a great scorer at North Carolina. His best season was 1983, when he scored 721 points for a 20 point per game average. In his third and last season, he scored 607 points in 31 games.*

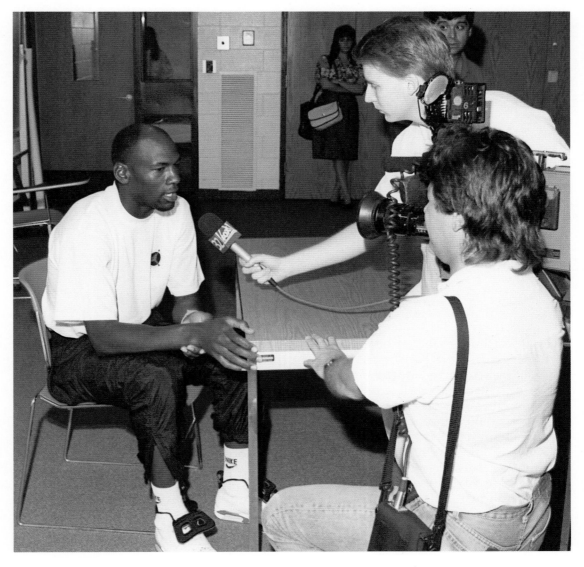

Right: *Jordan once heeded Dean Smith's advice to take a radio-TV course at North Carolina, and it paid rich dividends: Jordan has always displayed a unique ability to handle the media hordes with great style.*

director, still marvels at the ease with which the 21-year-old handled the crush, but believes that Michael's extroverted nature, and his ability to get along with people, made the burden easier to bear. "He was more patient than I would have been, and a key part of my business is being patient with incessant demands," Brewer said.

This is not to say that pressure didn't affect Jordan at times. At the start of his junior year, after all of the adulation of two previous seasons and a huge pre-season build-up, his shooting performance dipped under 50 percent; he was getting into foul trouble too often; and he was simply playing without the sponta-neity that had marked his first two seasons. He later admitted to trying too hard to make every play a spectacular one so he could live up to outside expectations.

He cured the problem with a heart-to-heart talk with his father, followed by a film session with Smith that revealed the stark difference in his play from his sophomore year. When the season resumed after the Christmas break, he was back to his old form, his shooting percentage soared to 55 percent, and he again was the offensive and defensive star of the nation's top-ranked team.

Jordan's career at North Carolina featured high-light after highlight. In 1982, he became the Tar Heels' only freshman starter, and only the fourth

frosh ever to start under Smith. He earned his keep with a 13.5 points per game average and the ACC Freshman of the Year award. However, he will always be remembered for his clutch shot that year that won the national championship in the final 15 seconds against a Georgetown team that featured center Patrick Ewing. After the game, Tar Heels assistant coach Eddie Fogler put everything into perspective when he said, "That kid has no idea of what he's just done. He's part of history but he doesn't know it yet."

Jordan became synonymous with The Shot, and really tired of hearing about it everywhere he went in the succeeding months. His attitude changed later. "That night, it all happened so fast that it just seemed like we had won another game and that was it. I didn't know how much it meant to people."

He was chosen to the All-America teams in both his sophomore and junior seasons. As a soph, he averaged 20 points per game and was named National Player of the Year by *The Sporting News*. The Tar Heels got off to a stumbling start that season, losing their first two games and teetering on the brink of a third straight loss, against Tulane. The Green Wave led by two points with four seconds to play, and all they needed to do was to make the inbounds pass and dribble out the clock for a monumental upset win. When two Tulane players collided trying to reach the inbounds pass, Jordan scooped up the loose ball and threw in a 30-foot shot to force an overtime and an eventual Carolina victory.

More Jordan last-minute heroics occurred that season when Maryland trailed the Tar Heels by a point with two seconds to play. The Terps' Chuck Driesell drove to the baseline and was about to sink the go-ahead basket when Jordan came from the top of the key to block the shot and save the victory. No wonder that Maryland's Adrian Branch noted afterward, "Guarding Jordan is dirty, dirty work."

The biggest matchup of the ACC that season featured Jordan and Virginia's seven-foot, four-inch All-America center Ralph Sampson, but Jordan was undaunted by Sampson's 10-inch height advantage.

Opposite bottom left: Jordan wore jersey number 9 as a starter on the 1984 U.S. Olympic team that was coached by Bobby Knight.

Opposite bottom right: Jordan scored 24 points in the 1984 Olympic title game against Spain before an injured ankle forced him out of the contest.

Right: Jordan celebrates the U.S. gold medal championship game victory over Spain at the 1984 Olympic Games in Los Angeles. He is one of the few players in basketball history to have won an NCAA championship, an NBA championship and an Olympic gold medal.

In the season's first meeting, Virginia was trying to come from behind when Sampson tried a five-foot hook shot. To his astonishment, Jordan blocked it. In the second game of the year between the two schools, Virginia led 63-60 with 67 seconds to play when Jordan tipped in a missed shot, then stole a pass and dunked another basket, and finally clinched the win by beating Sampson for the final rebound.

During his junior season, Jordan took on his "new look," shaving his head before a game against North Carolina State in which he cleaned the backboards for 12 rebounds and added 18 points. When the teams played again, he scorched the Wolfpack with 32 points. At Maryland and Wake Forest, he scored 36 points and had 17 rebounds, and then proceeded to score 20 or more points in 10 of his next dozen games. In his last 22 games, he averaged 21.7 points per game and 5.8 rebounds; shot 56.4 from the field; and

shot 78 percent from the foul line. He led the ACC with a 19.6 scoring average, finishing the year with 1788 points, ninth best in Tar Heel history, and for the second straight season was a unanimous All-America selection.

At the end of the 1984 season, Jordan skated through the vigorous trials for the U.S. Olympic team, coached by Indiana's Bobby Knight, and was the key player on what many considered the greatest U.S. Olympic team to that time. The team won all eight of its games by an average of 32 points, including a crushing 96-65 victory over Spain in the gold medal game in which Jordan led all scorers with 20 points.

With an NCAA championship and an Olympic gold medal stashed away during three momentous years, there were no more amateur fields left for Jordan to conquer. But there was plenty of gold out there in the NBA hills.

23

PART II
AIR JORDAN FLIES IN THE NBA

There is a fine line between luck and genius . . . and at times, there is no line at all, as Chicago Bulls general manager Jerry Krause realizes every time he sees Michael Jordan play basketball. In June 1984, Chicago had the third pick in the first round of the NBA draft and Krause, the team's personnel boss, knew that Jordan, having just been selected the best player in college basketball en route to a second consecutive first team All-America selection, and with an Olympic team berth awaiting him, was forgoing his senior year at North Carolina.

Nevertheless, Krause wanted dearly to draft Sam Bowie, an injury-plagued, seven-foot, one-inch center from the University of Kentucky, and he was bitterly disappointed when the Portland Trail Blazers, selecting just ahead of Chicago, drafted him. Thus, Krause became a reluctant suitor and felt "forced" to select Jordan. So much for genius.

In his first nine seasons at Chicago, he took the Bulls to three consecutive NBA championships (1991-92-93); tied Wilt Chamberlain's NBA record with seven consecutive scoring titles (Chamberlain got his in 1960-66 but never took his team to an NBA title during those years); became Chicago's all-time high scorer with more than 21,000 points; compiled a 33 points-per-game average that is the highest in NBA history; was the only player other than Wilt Chamberlain ever to score 3000 points in a single season (his 3041 points during the 1987 season was the third highest in league history); and has been a starter in the NBA All-Star game every year of his career.

Perhaps Krause should have talked to Jordan's father, James, during his contemplation process. If he had, there never would have been the slightest doubt had he factored in all that Michael had already achieved, abbetted by some basic family philosophy that James Jordan once related to an interviewer: "The way it is in our family is that we try to make something happen rather than waiting around for it to happen. We believe the surest way is to work toward making it the way you want it."

Opposite: *Jordan, with no other frontiers to conquer at North Carolina and with an Olympic gold medal tucked away, knew that stardom awaited him in professional basketball.*

Right: *Bulls general manager Rod Thorn signed Jordan to the richest NBA contract ever given to a rookie guard after Michael was the third player selected in the 1984 draft. Chicago really wanted Kentucky center Sam Bowie, who was selected just ahead of Jordan.*

Opposite: *Who else but Michael Jordan would win the 1988 NBA Slam Dunk Contest – the perfect stage for his talents.*

Above: *Jordan, always unselfish, then shared his $12,500 Slam Dunk winner's check with his teammates.*

Jordan's career both on and off the court has been truly remarkable. His success is unanimously hailed on the basketball court in terms of numbers, but a truer measure of just who Jordan is and why he has achieved such fame can be seen away from basketball, where he has so capably juggled his life to accommodate everyone and everything that spins into his orbit.

His teammates love him because he shares his own glory — as well as some of the rewards which accrue from it. When he won an NBA slam dunk contest, he divvied up the $12,500 first prize among his teammates. And moments after the Bulls won the NBA title in 1991, Michael insisted that the now-familiar "We're going to Disney World" refrain be uttered by the four other starters and that everyone split the $100,000 stipend. He appointed his parents as vice presidents of his mega-million-dollar conglomerate and made them an integral part of the post-game hoopla following Chicago's NBA title-clinching win over Los Angeles.

The public loves him, too. On Halloween in 1986, he posted a note on his front door telling trick-or-treaters that he would return in three days and to visit him at that time. He has always honored his older brother Larry by wearing Number 23, as close to half of the jersey number 45 that Larry wore as a high school player; he honors North Carolina by wearing his old UNC shorts under his uniform; and feels that he honors his sport by insisting on a "love of the game" clause in his contract that enables him to play the game anywhere he chooses in the off-season — and that usually means pick-up games with old friends back in North Carolina.

Worried that kids will imitate his habit of sticking out his tongue as he drives toward the basket to deposit one of his patented dunk shots, he always makes it a point to tell young audiences to avoid the temptation to do likewise for fear they might be hit and inadvertently bite into their tongues. It was the same advice that Dean Smith, his North Carolina coach, gave to him, but that habit had become so ingrained that Michael simply was unable to break it. Now, it has become as familiar a part of his persona as anything he does on the court.

On his way home after every Bulls home game in 1991, he stopped at a street corner in the run-down inner city area just four blocks from Chicago Stadium, and spent time talking with four neighborhood boys. He had met the lads the previous year as they waited in terrible weather outside the stadium, and had brought them into the arena. Some people wonder why he would bother to meet the same four kids each night and talk about anything they wish, but the reason is the essence of what makes Michael Jordan.

"If I don't stop," he has said, "I'll go home knowing they're waiting for me anyway. What does it cost me, a couple of minutes? It's on my way anyway and if I

Opposite: *Jordan uses several speeds en route to the basket with his long, thoroughbred-like stride. But regardless of which gear he is in, every swoop to the basket features that protruding tongue – a habit he developed as a young player and never has been able to change.*

Right: *"Don't do it,"* Jordan advises young players who may try to imitate his habit of sticking out his tongue whenever he goes up for a shot or a rebound. His biggest fear is that youngsters, trying to imitate his style, may unintentionally injure their tongues in a collision.

went home or went out to dinner knowing that they were standing there waiting and I hadn't shown up, it would ruin my evening."

The reasoning is similar to that which he once exercised with a TV interviewer who questioned the efficacy of kids wearing his patented *Air Jordan* sneakers "because they aren't going to turn into Michael Jordans."

"No," Jordan answered in his best disarming manner, "I tell 'em the first lesson: 'Don't be like me. Be better than me. That's the goal.'"

Jordan has always striven to be better. When he was in high school, he once took a home economics course because he felt so socially inept that he figured he'd be a lifelong bachelor. Today, he is married with a family but still is very self-sufficient around the house, according to his wife, Juanita. After the 1990 season, he was physically worn out and to prevent that from happening again, he purchased $40,000 worth of exercise equipment for his home and maintained a vigorous off-season program that returned a stronger, fresher Michael Jordan to the NBA wars. The payoff: His third NBA Most Valuable Player Award and a world championship.

He has carried the same dedication to his off-the-court enterprises, which net him more than $30 million per year, more than seven times his NBA salary. He has a talented staff of advisors to help him conduct these deals, in which he promotes a variety of products favored by young people, and which make

Above: *Jordan always has been generous with his time for kids, signing autographs, working at clinics, or just talking with them.*

Opposite: *"Air Jordan" athletic shoes by Nike became one of Jordan's most successful commercial ventures.*

him the most sought-after athlete in pro sports. Jordan's professional advisors melded his great college and Olympic achievements, along with his number one draft pick status, into a bevy of lucrative commercial interests before he had even sunk his first NBA basket.

"It took some getting used to, but now I enjoy the off-the-court stuff," Jordan has said. "It's like being back in school. I'm learning all the time. I've been given an opportunity to meet all kinds of people, to travel and expand my financial capabilities, to get ideas and learn about life, to create a world apart from basketball."

But his basketball world is the dynamic that sets the rest in motion, and everyone agrees that few ever have played the game better. Certainly, no player has ever performed with the flair that he has brought to the game. His swooping, driving, hang-in-the-air shots are a unique form of basketball ballet and acrobatics, providing an entertainment level never before seen in the NBA — not even in the days of Julius Erving, the famed Dr. J., with whom he has often been compared.

From the beginning of his NBA career, Jordan eschewed any comparisons to Erving, though admitting that Dr. J. had been his boyhood idol in style and that he had adapted some of it to his own game. "I'm more of a finesse player, a more fluid type of player," he said at the time. "He's taller than I am, much stronger and will muscle a player where I hang in the air and make some type of move to get a foul.

"Nobody can replace The Doctor," he added. "He was the epitome of class and defined the NBA for me. It's a challenge to try and emulate him, but it's not as if I have to go out of my way. Being Michael Jordan means acting the same as I always have."

But times – and Jordan – have changed, as he heard one night in Salt Lake City's Salt Palace after he slam-dunked a ball over Utah's six-foot, one-inch guard John Stockton, and a fan in the front row screamed at him, "Why don't you pick on someone your own size?"

The next time down the court, the six-foot, six-inch Jordan slammed a shot over six-foot, eleven-inch Melvin Turpin, then looked toward the fan who had

32

Opposite: *Jordan's unabashed number one fan is his wife Juanita, and both are renowned for their participation in charity fund raising events.*

Right: *"Knee high to a grasshopper," or certainly to his famous NBA-star father, is Jeffrey Jordan, seen here with his dad at a 1991 rally in Chicago's Grant Park that honored the NBA champion Bulls.*

Opposite: *Jordan is involved in a variety of commercial ventures, from sneakers to automobiles to his "cover boy" status on millions of Wheaties cereal boxes.*

Above right: *Jordan's off-court ventures aren't strictly product-driven; among other things, he spends a great deal of time at youth basketball camps.*

Right: *Jordan is probably the most sought-after professional athlete in the United States for charity events such as golf tournaments and other fund raisers.*

berated him and turned his palms upward, as if to say, "Is he big enough for you?"

Jordan once told an interviewer that he was incredulous when a veteran coach, noting that a layup is the highest percentage shot, once asked him why he went on "trying those outrageous jumps and moves and dunks."

"Hey, I don't plan this stuff. It just happens," he said to the coach, staring at him in disbelief.

Incredible as that may sound, Jordan, who claims never to have measured his vertical jump, has always maintained that when he sets sail on a dunk course, he really doesn't know how the trip will end. "I always spread my legs when I jump high, like on my rock-a-bye-baby dunk, and it seems like I've opened a parachute that slowly brings me back to the floor. I go up for a normal shot, but after that I don't have any plans," he has said. "I don't practice those moves. I don't know how I do them. It's amazing."

He once described a dunk that he made against Milwaukee that looked "like I'm taking off, like somebody put wings on me. I sometimes think, 'When does "jump" become "flying"?' I don't have the answer yet."

But as much as he enjoys his spectacular offensive displays, he takes even greater pleasure in playing defense. Part of the reason is that he had to work

harder on this phase of his game after coming to Chicago, particularly as he had to be forced to break a habit of roaming from his man because he had been allowed to freelance in college. Being named to the NBA's all defensive team six consecutive times (1988-93) has meant as much to him as his scoring championships. In 1986-87, he also was the first NBA player ever to exceed 200 steals — he had 236, and went over 200 each subsequent season — and his 125 blocked shots that year and 131 the following season were the most ever by a guard.

Jordan takes almost boyish delight in playing basketball, and some of this style has the marks of a kid. He pioneered the "baggy pants" look by tailoring his shorts an extra 2-½ inches longer, and now nearly every organized basketball team in the country wears its uniforms that way. He also honored his former college roommate and best friend Buzz Peterson, whose basketball career was cut short by a knee injury, by wearing a series of black and red (the Bulls' team colors) wristbands and knee braces. And of course, he has shaved his head so that it looks like a glistening ebony globe that acts as his personal homing beacon.

"People outside the sport always ask me how old I am," he has said. "They think I am older than my years and in my corporate involvement I try to project

myself as that old. In reality, I never want to grow up."

Despite his youthful exuberance, Jordan has always known his limitations. He knew from the start of his career with the Bulls that he was a dominant player, and though just 21 years old, he wasn't fooled by the lack of talent around him, nor by the fact that he was expected to provide most of the action, into thinking he could single-handedly create a championship team. His rookie performance led some skeptics, who recognized the Bulls' lack of supporting talent, to speculate that Jordan's offensive dominance did little to raise his teammates' confidence or performance levels. They cited the fact that both Larry Bird, in Boston, and Magic Johnson, in Los Angeles, had lifted their teams, an unfair argument because each of those players joined teams with far more talent than Jordan found in Chicago.

Jordan's dominance was cited as a problem even by the Bulls, once causing Krause to note: "Michael is a great player, probably the greatest player who ever played, but there are difficulties building [a team] around him. Because he's such a great competitor, even in practice, he tends to dominate his own teammates and that can, at times, disrupt practice in the same way that he disrupts opponents during games. Another thing is that his teammates have a tendency to stand around and watch him during games. They sort of have that 'let him do it' attitude. It's hard not be

Opposite: *Jordan's personal trademarks include different colored wrist bands and knee braces worn according to whether he is playing at home or away, and part of an old North Carolina uniform worn under his specially tailored uniform pants which are 2½ inches longer than normal.*

Above: *Jordan realized a boyhood dream during his rookie season when he matched his skills against his boyhood idol, Julius Erving.*

Right: *Like Erving, Jordan often was accused of being a "one-man team" — and it was essentially true, until the Bulls finally surrounded him with better players.*

mesmerized by him."

In Jordan's opinion, the crux of the problem lay elsewhere. Jordan always bridled at the "one-man team" tag, and was visibly angered upon once hearing an NBA player term him "the Bulls' only Division I prospect." He had more than a few skirmishes with Krause prior to the 1991 championship season over what he perceived to be the general manager's lack of purpose in supporting him with better players. For most of his time in Chicago after being drafted, Jordan believed management was content to allow him to carry the club by his own skills.

His frustration on this matter overflowed in 1988 when, after the Bulls were ousted by the Pistons in five games in the Eastern Conference playoffs, Jordan told reporters to go ask Krause — "don't ask me" — what the Bulls needed to become a winning team.

"Individually, I don't think I have a thing left to prove to anyone," he said. "All I'm interested in is winning. I would have to say that I'm pretty easy to build a team around because I can make contributions in all kinds of different ways — scoring, rebounding, passing. The one thing that I see that might make it tough

for the other players on the team is the amount of publicity that I receive. Because of that, people have a tendency to overlook the other players."

When Krause finally added Scottie Pippen, Horace Grant and Bill Cartwright to go with John Paxson — the Jordanaires, they were called, the name a take-off on a musical group from the 1950s — the Bulls finally became real contenders. Pippen has been a star in his own right in the Bulls' three NBA championships, and joined Jordan on the 1992 U.S. Olympic team, while Grant added rebounding and defensive strength to Chicago's inside game and helped Cartwright, who is only an average center but flourished with better talent around him. The net result was that Jordan produced as never before in this new team concept and responded by raising the abilities of everyone on the team.

While the acquisition of improved players underscored the logic of Jordan's reasoning, the Bulls' foes remained especially wary of Jordan, who had proved early on that he was easily capable of exploding for 40 or 50 points and carrying his teammates to victory. The Lakers' Michael Cooper, one of the NBA's best

Right: Jordan felt more comfortable surrounded by a supporting cast that came to be known as the Jordanaires – Scottie Pippen, Horace Grant, Bill Cartwright and John Paxson – which became the nucleus that helped the Bulls to the 1991 NBA championship.

Right: Jordan is so talented that he can raise the supporting cast around him to even higher performance levels. Cartwright, who came to the Bulls in a trade, was considered only an average center until he played with Jordan, while Pippen's game improved to the point where he is considered ready for NBA star status.

Left: *Jordan always attracts a crowd when he has the ball, as happened in the 1991 NBA Eastern Conference finals when Dennis Rodman, Tree Rollins (30) and Joe Dumars (4) of the Detroit Pistons tried to keep him from scoring.*

Opposite top: *Jordan always plays basketball with a variety of emotions and he never has hesitated to hide them, whether it be impatience (left) or enthusiasm as he encourages his teammates in the locker room or during a game (right).*

Opposite bottom: *Remarkably, Jordan always manages to crystallize his feelings into very clear, concise thoughts, making him very popular with the media during the blizzard of interviews that he must undergo. Here, he gives his first interview as a member of the Chicago Bulls.*

defensive players during most of the 1980s who always was credited with doing the best job defending Jordan, declared that no one player could shut him down.

"When people say I, or some other player, shut him down, that's wrong," he said. "There's no way I can stop him. I need the whole team and so does every other player who takes him on. As soon as he touches the ball, he electrifies you. The alarm goes off because you don't know what he's going to do. He goes right, left, over you, around and under you. He twists, he

turns. And you know he's going to get the shot off. You just don't know when and how. That's the most devastating thing psychologically to a defender."

On the other hand, Jordan certainly has been a psychological boost for his teammates. He doesn't worry about being a good guy but is a relentless leader – in practice, on the court during a game, and in the locker room. He has a likeable personality and a good sense of humor, but he doesn't worry about being the closest friend of everyone on the team.

Bulls coach Phil Jackson calls him "a challenge type

of guy", and whenever Jordan believes any of his mates are not producing as they should, he will not hesitate to chew on them, particularly when the errors are mental or from lack of intensity. Even when his chewings occur as a result of his own frustrations, his teammates never have expressed any resentment.

"As a leader, I have never been critical or cursed any of my teammates," he said. "I've always spoken in terms of 'we'."

Sometimes he adds his own bit of emphasis — a kicked chair or water cooler — but always in the context of trying to stir his mates. He never mentions names, but all agree he never has to because players know when they are not fully performing. Jordan only gets upset when he believes players don't give as much as he did in a game, and if the lack of effort and concentration results in a loss, he is most likely to explode.

In the 1990 Eastern Conference finals, he fired out at his teammates during halftime of the second game, and again after the team had lost that game to go down 2-0 in the series. It worked, because Chicago came back to tie the series, though they eventually lost in seven games.

Jordan knew when he came to the Bulls in 1984 that there would be frustrations, because winning teams usually don't have the third pick in the draft. Yet the choice was as much a boon for Jordan as it was for Chicago because, had the Portland Trail Blazers selected him over Bowie, his skills may well

Opposite: Jordan helped the Bulls recoup the $4 million they paid him for his first contract from the very start – his great style was such an instant hit in Chicago that attendance at Bulls games doubled in his first season.

Right: During his rookie season, Jordan made a shambles of a scouting report that listed his liabilities. He was named NBA Rookie of the Year while also making the NBA's All-Rookie team after he averaged 28.2 points, had 481 assists and 196 steals.

not have flourished. At the time, the Blazers already had a surplus of small forwards and big guards with players such as Jim Paxson, Clyde Drexler and Kiki Vanderweghe.

Thus, Jordan had the same opportunity afforded Larry Bird and Magic Johnson in 1979 – to make an immediate impact on a franchise and a city. There were differences, though, because those players were the new jewels in already-rich basketball crowns, while Jordan joined a team that had won just 27 and 28 games in each of the previous two seasons, and had almost given up hope of ever winning an NBA title. Chicago had been in one post-season playoff series in the previous seven years and were at rock-bottom in fan acceptance, having finished the 1984 season with their second-worst average attendance.

Jordan changed all of that. He had signed a five-year contract worth $4 million, the highest for a guard in NBA history, but the Bulls began recouping their investment immediately. Within one season, home attendance doubled and the TV audience added 30,000 households; and within three seasons, the Bulls attracted over 650,000 home fans and added another 39 percent to attendance increases on the road. In that third season, the added attendance at Bulls games accounted for one-third of the NBA's total increase.

Jordan was an immediate sensation, starting with the exhibition games when he led the team in scoring in six of the seven games while playing an average of 29 minutes. In just his second pre-season game, he hit 10 of 11 field goals and 12 of 13 fouls in a 107-100 win over the Kansas City Kings. During the season Jordan immediately vied with Bird and Johnson as the NBA's hottest gate attraction. In his third regular season game, against Milwaukee, he scored 37 points, and then scored 45 against San Antonio in his eighth game while scoring 25 or more points in 10 of his first 15 starts. In Oakland, fans called for the Bulls to reinstate Jordan in a game, even though it jeopardized the hometown Golden State Warriors' chances for a victory; and in Los Angeles, Jordan faced the woeful Clippers and the game outdrew the Lakers in head-to-head competition that night. Even actor Jack Nicholson, the Lakers' alleged Number 1 fan, deserted his favorite team to watch Jordan. He wasn't disappointed: Michael tied the game at 100-100 with an 18-foot jump shot; threw up a scoop shot on a breakaway though he was grabbed from behind and held by Clippers' guard Derek Smith; and then saved the Bulls' win by stealing the ball on the Clippers' final possession.

Through all of this, Jordan made a shambles of an NBA scouting report that said defenses should play

him to drive to the basket; that he couldn't go to his left with the ball; and that he didn't shoot well from the outside. "They didn't know about my first step or the moves or the jump," Jordan said at the time. "They based everything on my college performances. But during the Olympics, I improved my overall game, including my outside shooting, because Coach (Bobby) Knight helped me to concentrate and do things without a lot of lollygagging around. So I knew I was taking everybody by surprise, including myself, when that first NBA season began."

Actually, Jordan had gotten a taste of what awaited him in the NBA during his days with the Olympic team. He had already begun to spin some of his magic during a series of exhibition games against teams comprised of NBA players, and during the pre-game warmup before a game in Indianapolis, an Olympic team's practice ball bounced to the pros' end of the court. Jordan chased after it and Bird picked it up. Instead of handing it to him, the Celtics star sneered and kicked it back over his head. "Bird was showing me it was all business now, and I was beneath him," Jordan said. "I didn't forget."

He didn't let his NBA opponents forget, either. Few had ever seen a player with such quickness, causing Indiana Pacers guard Jim Thomas to note, "I don't know if his first step toward the basket is legal because I've never had time to judge it."

His jumping ability caused a Bulls' assistant coach to note: "He has more hang time than (Oakland Raiders kicker) Ray Guy."

On his shooting, Darrell Walker of the Knicks noted: "The really amazing thing is that when he gets his shot off, it's so soft."

Still, Jordan went through the same learning process that any college star must endure, but the key to his survival was in not allowing the pressure to bother him. "At Carolina, I was in a controlled system, and a lot of the crowd was pleased with my play," he said. "So, in the NBA, if I played my natural game, I didn't have any problems with the crowd. Actually, it was the most relaxed time of my career to that point because while there were more games, they came so quickly that if I had a bad one, I could quickly put the past behind me and get ready for the present."

In his rookie season, Jordan led the NBA in points with 2313; helped the Bulls to 11 more victories than they had had the previous season, and to a playoff berth; and was selected as Rookie of the Year. Those results helped Jordan to stake a place for himself among pro basketball's elite. It was only left for him to grow as a player, and to gain stature as a star. But he was set back in the third game of his second season when he broke a bone in his left foot and missed the next 64 games.

For the first time, the NBA got a look at the "other"

Right: *Larry Bird sent a message to Jordan about life in the NBA by kicking a stray ball instead of handing it to him during a practice game for the 1984 Olympics. From the start, their on-the-court rivalry was one of the NBA's most intense.*

Below and below right: *"Hang time" was once something only attributed to football punters, but Jordan brought the term to the NBA with his incredible ability to hang in the air while shooting and seeming to stay there long after the ball had left his hands.*

Jordan — the competitive, combative Jordan. As the inactivity continued, Jordan by his own admission was "going crazy," because the doctors forbade him even to practice until the bone was completely healed. In February, he returned to the University of North Carolina, telling the Bulls he was going to take more credits toward his degree in geography (he eventually did graduate). In reality, he returned to play pickup games with his friends because he simply couldn't tolerate the inactivity, particularly when he felt the broken bone was healed. When Jordan returned to Chicago a month later and declared himself fit enough to play, the doctors still demurred, saying the bone was only 90 percent healed.

As the season wound down to its final month, Jordan, over the objections of his agent who wanted him to sit out the entire season, all but bullied the Bulls into allowing him to suit up while limiting his playing time at first to seven minutes a half, then gradually increasing it. In those final 15 games, Jordan unleashed the volcano of frustration that had seethed within him for over nearly five months, helping Chicago to get the last playoff berth. He averaged 22.7 points, just two fewer than during the first three games prior to his injury.

In the playoffs, he turned in one of the most magnificent performances ever seen in an NBA game when he scored a record-setting 63 points in a double overtime loss to the Celtics at Boston Garden, after having scored 49 points in the first game of the series. It was a classic shootout duel — Jordan vs. Larry Bird (who scored 36 points and had more all-around support from a far more talented team). Michael single-handedly kept his underdog Bulls in the game, and at the conclusion of the 135-131 Boston victory, Bird issued his now-famous proclamation about Jordan's ability: "I think it's just God disguised as Michael Jordan."

The previous playoff scoring record was 61 points by Los Angeles Lakers Hall of Famer Elgin Baylor, to whom Jordan has been favorably compared, against the Celtics more than two decades earlier. Ironically, it was Jordan's defense that sent the game into overtime and gave him an opportunity to break that hallowed mark. With nine seconds to play in regulation

Left: *Jordan broke his foot in the third game of the 1986 season, and when he returned for the final 15 games he blew off months of frustration by averaging nearly 23 points a game and helping the team to the last playoff berth.*

Opposite: *The Bird-Jordan rivalry peaked during the 1986 playoffs when Jordan scored an NBA playoff record 63 points during a double overtime loss against Bird and the Celtics. Bird had 36 points but he also had stronger support.*

46

Above: *"I think it's just God disguised as Michael Jordan," Larry Bird said after Jordan's 63 points against Boston in the 1986 playoffs.*

Opposite: *Michael and Magic on the court in 1985* (top left) *and 1990* (top right), *and off the court in 1991* (bottom right); *Jordan with rival Isiah Thomas in 1989* (bottom left).

early NBA career, it really was Jordan against the world because he did not have the strong supporting cast enjoyed by Bird in Boston, Magic Johnson in Los Angeles or Isiah Thomas in Detroit.

After Magic Johnson retired amid much publicity in 1991, Jordan replaced him as the darling of Madison Avenue's Ad Agency Row. In an era where marketability is measured by single name recognition (Johnson was always "Magic"), there is now only one "Michael."

Jordan is not unlike his former rival, a very outgoing person who is secure in a mob of autograph seekers, and is able, win or lose, to present a pleasant public persona while at the same time being very forthright with his opinions. However, he resents being a ripe target for stories built on rumor and innuendo, though he understands that his visibility causes this to happen. Occasionally, he displays his disgust publicly, as happened during the 1993 playoffs when he was the subject of questionable stories about his gambling activities. He shunned the media for a week before stating his case on national television, and then made himself available without recrimination.

Jordan did have an ongoing rivalry of sorts with both Magic Johnson and Isiah Thomas for most of his early years in the NBA. It had its genesis in Jordan's first All-Star game in 1985, when he believed that both players were part of a "conspiracy" to deny him the ball in the showcase game — he scored just seven points in 22 minutes. Even though Johnson was on the opposing team, Jordan felt that he was culpable because he didn't try to sidetrack the effort, which he believed was masterminded by Thomas. He became certain of its validity when Charles Tucker, the East Lansing, Michigan, psychologist and advisor to both Johnson and Thomas, said the two players were, in fact, chuckling about having taught Jordan a lesson.

Because Thomas and Johnson have always been close friends, they were linked in Jordan's mind as being against him. When the affair became public, Thomas met with Jordan before the Bulls and Pistons played each other two days later and tried to clear the air. But his plea fell on deaf ears, because Jordan termed it "mostly show," and then he exacted some revenge when he torched Detroit for 49 points in a Chicago victory.

Jordan snubbed Johnson's all-star game in Los Angeles for several years, but Johnson tried to remain above the fray and was always effusive in his public comments about Jordan. He once told a Hollywood TV producer that "everyone always says it's me and Larry (Bird) but really, it's Mike and everybody else." Finally, to his credit, Magic ended one half of this "feud," when he approached Jordan to square matters in 1987. "We can't be separated like this," Johnson told him. "I respect you too much, and I'm sure you respect me."

That cleared the air between the two of them, and though they may never be best friends, they became friendly rivals. In the 1991 NBA finals, both were excited at the prospect of facing down each other for the world championship — which the Bulls won in five

time, and with Boston leading 116-114, he stripped the ball from center Robert Parish and launched a three-point shot that bounced off the rim. But Celtic Kevin McHale fouled him, and Jordan hit both shots, his 53rd and 54th points, to force overtime.

Thanks to Jordan's relentless play, the game lasted two overtime periods. He scored nine points, and the last two — a swooping drive over the seven-foot Parish — broke Baylor's record. "Michael was doing so much, so well, that I found myself just wanting to stop and watch him — and I was playing," his fellow guard, John Paxson said afterward, adding: "I'm sure there are heads over in the Celtics locker room who can't believe the things he did today."

Much was made of the Jordan-Bird rivalry in that game, but that was true only in the context of two superstars trying to help their teams win. During his

games – and Johnson said he was disappointed that the ultimate bit of theater didn't result in a seventh-game duel. "I fantasized that it would have been the kind of thing where the other guys would step aside and watch us play," he said.

Jordan went through a lot of pain and suffering to reach that plateau, despite some great moments over the next few seasons. In the first game of the 1987 season in New York, his 50 points set a Madison Square Garden record for an opposing player — remarkable considering that the history of the NBA, with all of its great players, really centered around this storied arena. He scored his team's final 11 points and 21 of its final 31 in a comeback 108-103 victory over the Knicks. The next night in Cleveland, he scored the last eight points in Chicago's 94-89 win, and two nights after that, he got 34 in a 111-104 win against San Antonio.

Later that season, Jordan scored 40 points 11 times in a 12-game stretch, and finished the season with

3041 points, joining Wilt Chamberlain as the only player ever to exceed 3000 in a season — and the first non-seven-footer ever to do it. His 37.1 scoring average not only led the NBA that year, but it was also the fifth highest in NBA history (Chamberlain had the other four marks). He had 50 or more points in three consecutive games, and the highlight of the season came when he scored 23 straight points against the Atlanta Hawks. He also became the first NBA player ever to have more than 200 steals and 100 blocked shots in a season — his 125 total blocked shots exceeded the total of 13 of the league's starting centers.

Jordan hit his stride toward superstardom in 1988 when he finally was recognized as being a complete player, and not simply a point-scorer. He was chosen the NBA's Most Valuable Player for the first time after winning his second straight scoring title, with 2868 points, for a 35 points per game average. That was but one of many honors, which also included his second straight first team selection on the all-league team,

and his selection as MVP of the All-Star game for the first time.

He took even more glee in the emergence of his all-around game, as he was named NBA Defensive Player of the Year for the first time while earning a place on the all-NBA defensive team. "I enjoy playing defense even more than offense," he said, "and I wish I could concentrate more on that phase of the game." Michael underscored his defensive ability by leading the NBA with 259 steals, and suddenly the Bulls' foes faced the dilemma of the "800-pound gorilla" syndrome because he had become a force that had to be reckoned with at both ends of the court.

Midway through the 1989 season, he agreed to shift from the off-, or shooting, guard spot to point guard, where he would control the ball, and the critics were highly skeptical of that move. But he silenced them quickly during a streak of 10 straight games when he compiled triple doubles (double figures in scoring, rebounding and assists), achieving this rare feat in 12 of the team's final 24 games while playing at that position. Since then, there has not been a better all-around point guard in the NBA.

Best of all, he got a kick out of the switch. "I think people could see what happened to this team when I went to point guard," he said. "It was a challenge that I enjoyed because the point guard's job is to distribute the ball to his teammates; to be a leader which, in effect, makes him like another coach on the floor. That's what I wanted to do even though I had played the off-guard position all my life and it's really my natural position."

The switch also energized his teammates. He got them all involved with his passing and direction, and with increased defensive attention, talented players such as Pippen, Grant, B. J. Armstrong, and Cartwright all benefitted by having better shooting opportunities.

The immediate result for Jordan was not only a third straight scoring title, but also a selection as NBA Player of the Year by more than a two-to-one margin over his rival, Magic Johnson. All of this caused New York Knicks coach Rick Pitino to note, "He's the best I've ever seen. I played college ball with Julius Erving and I've watched Magic, but the thing about Michael is that he really doesn't have a weakness."

Cleveland guard Craig Ehlo voiced almost the same opinion after Jordan's nearly impossible buzzer-beating shot knocked the Cavaliers out of the playoffs that year. "He gives me nightmares," Ehlo said, and the Pistons felt the same way for a while as Chicago then jumped to a 2-1 lead in the Eastern Conference finals before bowing out in six games to the eventual world champions.

Jerry Krause finally answered Jordan's pleas and rebuilt the Bulls for the 1990 season, putting on the floor a quicker, more athletic and deeper team than had been beaten by Detroit in the previous playoffs. He also changed coaches, elevating assistant Phil Jackson over Doug Collins, with whom Jordan did not get along.

Now there was nothing left to do but relax and play basketball, and Michael had a blast as he led the Bulls to 55 victories, including a powerful 35-6 mark at home. Jordan averaged nearly 34 points a game and had a mighty 69-point splurge in a 117-113 overtime victory over Cleveland, the ninth best scoring feat in NBA history, en route to his fourth straight NBA scoring title. Jordan, with better people around him, also altered his offensive style a bit, relying more on a perimeter jump shot and less on his patented drives to the basket.

"It was my best season ever from a team standpoint," he said. "There were seasons when I grabbed more rebounds or scored more points, but from the point of view of making a total contribution, this was the best."

After eliminating Milwaukee in the first playoff round, Jordan ripped through the Philadelphia 76ers with startling ease, averaging 43 points per game, and scoring 49 points in one game and 45 in two others. When pundits measured his duel against the Sixers' Charles Barkley, Jordan won easily by outscoring him 215-119. When Jordan measured the series, he called it his best playoff ever, noting, "I've never played so many consecutive games so well."

Once again, the Bulls faced the Pistons for the conference title and many believed that Chicago might prevail, based on their torrid showing against Philly. That's how it started in Game 1, as Jordan scored 14 of his team's first 20 points and had 26 at halftime. But the Pistons, renowned for their physical game, sent him crashing to the floor early in the second half and he came up hobbling with an injured hip that so hampered his play that he scored just eight points in the second half as the Bulls lost 86-77.

In reality, the series was lost right there, because the Bulls fell behind 2-0 after losing the second game when no one stepped forward to pick up the tempo, and by the time he had regained his form with a 47-point third game to help Chicago win, the cushion they needed was lost. The series went to a seventh game — a game the Bulls felt never would have been played had Jordan been healthy in the first two games — but Jordan could not do it alone, despite scoring 31 points. A severe migraine headache made Pippen ineffective, Paxson was out with an injured ankle, and all of the Bulls, except for Jordan, had horrible shooting nights.

When the 1991 season rolled around, there was a different feeling around the Bulls, and it all flowed from Jordan. He copped a fifth straight scoring title with a 31.5 average, started every game, and had a litany of scoring milestones including his 15,000th

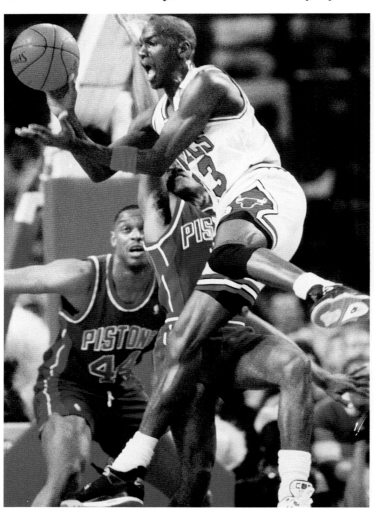

point, scored at Philadelphia, the second fastest achievement (Chamberlain was first) at that level; his 500th blocked shot; a season-high 46 points against Milwaukee; and 30 or more points 52 times while leading the team in scoring in 75 of its 82 games. All of this not only helped him become the leading candidate for the All-Star game, but also earned him the NBA's Most Valuable Player award at the end of the season.

But despite all the records, all the points, and all the honors, Jordan liked nothing better than leading the Bulls to the 1991 NBA championship — in almost blitzkrieg fashion over the Los Angeles Lakers and his now-friendly rival, Magic Johnson — for which he also was named finals MVP after compiling a 31.2 average, 11 assists, and nearly seven rebounds per game.

But first, there was a bit of unfinished business against the Pistons in the conference finals, accomplished in a stunning four-game sweep that totally humiliated the defending NBA champions. That sweep also accentuated the depth of Jordan's feud with Isiah Thomas, who, along with a couple of his mates, walked off the court before the final whistle of the last game without staying to congratulate Jordan or the other Bulls players, as is always customary in such instances.

Page 53: *The classic Jordan move – past the defender (Cleveland's Mark Price), tongue out and body in full drive toward the basket.*

Right: *Opposing defense can't always assure themselves that Jordan will drive to the basket, because he has become such a prolific scorer that he will stop and pop from any spot on the floor.*

Jordan and his mates countered the Pistons' roughhouse and garbage-talking tactics with some of their own, and that so unnerved Detroit that they became a fumbling, bumbling team starkly contrasted against the smooth-working Bulls. In Game 3, for example, Chicago had built a 24-8 lead and a trapping defense forced center James Edwards to handle the ball in the center of the court where he is least comfortable. Jordan roared in and jumped completely over the six-foot, eleven-inch player and swatted the ball away, leading to a quick transition jumper by Paxson. Michael finished that game with 33 points, 14 of which were in the final period, along with a great display of defense typical of that which had already earned him another berth on the NBA's all-defensive team. It also sounded the death knell for Detroit, as Chicago easily eliminated them 115-94 in the fourth game before their home fans.

Jordan finally had his chance to play for an NBA title, and fans everywhere played up the Michael vs. Magic duel, though the two would actually be matched against each other only on sporadic occasions. Jordan stepped to the fore not only with his all-around play, but also with his aggressive leadership. When the Bulls lost the first game, he singled out Paxson for missing four open shots, so in the second game, the Bulls' "other" guard hit all eight of his shots as Chicago erupted with a blazing 38-point third quarter en route to a 107-86 victory. Jordan hit 15 of 18 field goals, and had 13 assists and seven rebounds.

Best of all in that game was a move that even astounded him: He drove to the basket, raised the ball as if to dunk with his right hand, but when he saw the Lakers' Sam Perkins move over to block his path, he switched the ball to his left hand and sank an underhanded scoop shot.

When the series moved to Los Angeles, Jordan found himself closely guarded by Byron Scott (with plenty of help from other Lakers every time he touched the ball) and the Lakers built a 67-54 lead in the third quarter. Unlike past years, Jordan's teammates responded and eight different players each scored a basket – Jordan got only two foul shots during this run – and the Bulls tied the score. But with the game on the line, he sank a 14-foot jump shot with 3.4 seconds to play to send it into overtime; and then sealed the win with a steal, a feed to Paxson for a basket, two consecutive layups of his own and two free throws in a 104-96 victory.

Jordan came out of that game with a badly mashed right toe, and after experimenting for the first six minutes of Game 4 with a small hole in his sneaker to alleviate some of the pressure, he went back to his regular sneakers and took off like Air Jordan. He hit a jumper just before halftime to give Chicago a 52-44 lead; and in the third quarter, he either scored or assisted on seven of Chicago's 10 field goals as they built a 16-point lead.

Jordan became the Bulls' orchestrator as the Lakers double-teamed him, and he constantly fed the ball to Pippen, who scored 32 points, and to Paxson, who broke it open with a succession of long range

jump shots that accounted for 10 points in the final four minutes as Chicago went on to a 108-101 victory.

The Michael-Magic duel was decided in Jordan's favor as he consistently outscored his rival; matched him as a playmaker, which was Johnson's strong suit; and was easily the most dominating player during the entire series.

Jordan repeated the same scenario in 1992 and 1993 when the Bulls became only the third team ever to win three consecutive NBA titles, and the first to do it since the Boston Celtics ran off eight straight in the 1960s. He also became the first player ever to win three consecutive playoff MVP awards.

In between, he won his second Olympic gold medal, at the 1992 Summer Olympics in Barcelona as a member of America's famed "Dream Team," so called because 11 of its 12 members were among the greatest stars from the NBA. As was the case eight years earlier, he quietly dominated the team with his great all-round play, but kept a reasonably low profile among a group of millionaire athletes whose presence dominated the Olympic games. Yet Jordan couldn't help but be *the* player everyone came to see.

Working at guard with Magic Johnson, he was the "finisher" with his swooping, flying dunks when Magic triggered the fast break; when Jordan ran the offense, it was controlled yet spiced with a few no-look passes; and when coach Chuck Daly wanted to defense his opponent's best player, he turned to Jordan. He shut down Golden State Warriors star Sarunas Marciulionis who played for Lithuania, when that team made a run at the U.S. in a semi-final game; and turned in a key defensive job against Croatia's six-foot, ten-inch Tony Kukoc in a 117-85 victory over Croatia in the gold medal game, in which he also led the team with 22 points.

None of the riches or other distractions of superstardom have affected Jordan's ability to play the game at the highest level, because he is psychologically consumed by a need to dominate an opponent — any opponent, even his 1992 Olympic coach Chuck Daly, during a game of golf.

One afternoon during the Games, Jordan lost a golf match by one stroke to Daly, and fumed when Daly refused a rematch. At the crack of dawn the next day, Jordan phoned Daly seeking to change his mind.

When the phone went unanswered, he went to Daly's hotel room and pounded on the door until the coach answered, and refused to leave until he got his rematch. This time Jordan won by a stroke, and the two then agreed to live with the split.

That great competitive spirit has always been Jordan's hallmark on the basketball court, particularly if he feels personally challenged by another great player. First, it was Magic Johnson when the Bulls blew away the Lakers in the 1991 Finals; then fellow Dream Team teammates Clyde Drexler of the Portland Trail Blazers, in the 1992 Finals, and Charles Barkley

of the Phoenix Suns in 1993. He won the NBA's Most Valuable Player award in 1992, but finished third to Barkley in 1993. That just goaded him to demonstrate, in the 1993 Finals, who was truly the MVP with a dominating performance in head-to-head competition during which he scored 40 or more points in five of the six games while displaying a suffocating defense on any Suns player who seemed a threat. Dan Majerle, who had torched Chicago with six three-point field goals in Game 3 and hit two quick ones to close the first half of Game 4 that demolished a nine-point Bulls lead, was virtually shut down in the

Page 57: *Jordan holds up a victory sign as he stands on the podium with fellow Dream Team teammates Scottie Pippen (l) and Clyde Drexler after the U.S. beat Croatia for the gold medal at the 1992 Summer Olympics.*

Right: *Clyde Drexler of the Portland Trail Blazers once again became the enemy in the 1992 NBA finals. The Bulls won in six games.*

second half by Jordan, who limited him to a pair of harmless two-point field goals as Chicago won the game.

Jordan's contributions to the Bulls' victories in the NBA Finals to secure their second and third titles were almost replicas of each other. Each series lasted six games; Jordan almost singlehandedly won three of the games in each series while leading all scorers, and dominated the final decisive moments of each sixth game.

Against the Trail Blazers in 1992, the Bulls trailed by 17 points late in the third quarter of the sixth game, yet won 97-93. Jordan scored 33 points in that game, including 12 – and the game's last six – in the fourth quarter.

In the deciding game against Phoenix in 1993, the Bulls didn't score a point in the first six minutes of the last quarter and blew an eight-point lead. Jordan then told his teammates that he would take care of the scoring, and scored the next 12 points, including a

Left: *Michael Jordan displays his classic concentration and enthusiasm during the 1993 playoffs.*

crucial coast-to-coast drive that cut the Suns' lead to two points with less than 40 seconds to play. Jordan then started the play that led to John Paxson's game-winning three-point basket with less than four seconds remaining, and finished the 99-98 victory with 33 points, eight rebounds and a team-high seven assists in 44 minutes.

He had served notice of his intentions earlier in the 1993 playoffs, when he scored the winning basket at the buzzer in the final game of a four-game sweep against Cleveland; and against New York in the Eastern Conference finals when with his team down 0-2, he ripped off 54 points to even the series in Game 4, and followed with steady 29- and 25-point games that Chicago used to clinch the title with four consecutive wins.

When the Suns and Bulls tapped off for their championship series in 1993, Barkley was a media darling because of his outrageous behavior and penchant for colorful quotes. But Jordan's phenomenal all-round play was even more astounding than it had been in past series, and he totally dominated every phase of

play during the six games. He had averaged nearly 40 minutes a game during the regular season, then upped that to more than 45 minutes during the 19 playoff games. Though Phoenix rotated three defenders against him, he averaged an NBA Finals record 41 points per game, including 55 points in a 111-105 victory in Game 5. In fact, he was so dominating that the Suns said they were pleased to "hold" him to 41 points in one of their victories. Still, they couldn't keep him from averaging almost nine rebounds and seven assists in each game, or prevent him from scoring 40 or more points in five of the six games.

After Horace Grant blocked an attempt for a game-winning shot by the Suns' Kevin Johnson in the last second of the final contest, Jordan also had the presence of mind to escape the on-court celebration long enough to retrieve the game ball that was rolling loose under the basket. During a barrage of interviews in the Bulls' locker room after the game, he cradled it to his chest as lovingly as he had held the Bulls' first NBA championship trophy back in 1991.

That trophy was barely in place in the Bulls offices when Jordan's life turned upside down.

Within two months, his father James was found murdered in a South Carolina swamp, and two months after that, he announced his retirement from the NBA.

Michael was devastated by his father's death. James Jordan had become Michael's almost constant companion during the season and throughout the playoffs. Friends said they were more like brothers than father and son.

Suddenly his family, which he more or less took for granted during his halcyon NBA career, became his top priority. He was determined to reknit the Jordan family as tightly as possible – and nothing, not even basketball, would interfere.

Long before this tragedy, Michael's own emotional state was becoming threadbare because of the mental fatigue the game had exacted. Playing in the 1992 Olympic Games severely cut the off-season time that was so necessary for him to refuel emotionally after a gruelling season; within a few weeks of his triumph in Barcelona, he was back to the NBA grind.

During the 1993 season, Jordan told many of his teammates that it would be his final year. They scoffed and said such a stance was only to establish a superior bargaining position for a new contract. He was in the midst of an eight-year, $26 million deal that was a pittance compared to what many of the NBA's younger players, less talented and certainly without his achievements, were being paid.

On October 6, 1993, shortly before the Bulls were scheduled to report to training camp, Jordan announced his retirement before a jammed press conference that was televised worldwide. "I just feel that I don't have anything else to prove," he said at the time, adding: "The desire just isn't there." He also talked about his increasing lack of privacy and his grief over his father's death. But in true Jordan fashion, he also left open the possibility that he might

return. "I never say never to anything," he replied when asked if he never again would play in the NBA.

In the background and out of sight of most observers had been his father's suggestions after his first NBA title that he quit the NBA and give baseball a shot. James Jordan had persisted with the suggestion, and eventually Michael went to Jerry Reinsdorf, who owned both the Bulls and the Chicago White Sox, and got access to the batting cage at Comiskey Park. He soon placed an order for bats and began working

Opposite left: *Sir Charles tries to get in Michael's way in the 1993 NBA finals.*

Opposite right: *Jordan clutches the game ball as teammate Trent Tucker embraces him when the Bulls defeated the Phoenix Suns for their third NBA championship in a row.*

Above right: *Jordan's number 23 hung in the rafters of Chicago's United Center after he retired.*

Right: *Jordan wore jersey number 45 during his baseball stint and when he returned to the Bulls, until he "unretired" his old number 23 during the 1995 playoffs.*

in the cage, trying to resurrect skills that had lain dormant since his Laney High School days, when he had been as talented playing baseball as he had been on the basketball court. He had wanted to play the game at North Carolina, but the length of the basketball season didn't allow for a two-sport career.

After the 1993 season, Jordan was set to test the game briefly at the White Sox farm team in Hickory, North Carolina, but his father's death cancelled that move.

Then, almost as if to fulfill his father's wishes, Michael decided to pursue a professional baseball career with the White Sox. He reported to spring training in Florida in 1994 with more fanfare than any rookie in the game's history.

Everything – batting and fielding practice, hitting instruction, running the bases, the car he drove and of course, his play in the exhibition game – was fully chronicled in every form of media.

So was reaction and opinion. Realists, including Jordan, knew he had a long and difficult road to travel; and that group, with the exception of Michael who always had unbridled confidence in his ability to conquer any athletic challenge, believed it was the longest of long shots.

He was, after all, 31 years old, an age when many baseball players' careers either are on the downslide or already finished. Certainly, there were very few minor league players that age still trying to make it to the big leagues, and none who had not played the game for 13 years and who faced at least two or three more years in the minor leagues.

The overall reaction to Jordan's move ran the gamut from heavy doses of mean-spirited cynicism to very healthy skepticism. Few in the media gave him credit for trying either to reclaim his baseball skills or

Left: *When Jordan returned to the NBA with 17 games to play in the 1995 regular season, he hardly looked as if he had missed 21 months of NBA competition, leading his team in scoring 12 times and helping it coast into the playoffs.*

Opposite top right: *Though Jordan was a one-man gang for the Bulls during the 1995 playoffs, averaging more than 30 points in nine games, he sometimes tried to do too much, as happened here when he made an errant pass trying to get the Bulls a last-minute tie to avoid being eliminated by Orlando.*

for having the opportunity to pursue every man's dream of playing major league baseball.

The White Sox sent Michael to Birmingham of the Class A Southern League and he struggled through the 1994 season with a .202 batting average. He hit three home runs and drove in 51 in 127 games. When the season ended, he willingly went to the Winter Instructional League in Arizona, and upped his batting mark 35 points.

Jordan made his teammates in Birmingham feel special. Unlike other minor league teams, the Birmingham team traveled in a specially equipped, $750,000 luxury bus that Michael purchased. He made himself be just one of the team and never flouted his exalted status as he, like them, struggled to get better. In his off hours, he good-naturedly accepted their challenges for pickup basketball games.

Those games also had an unintended effect, because they kept alive his interest in the game. He showed he had maintained his great skills during an All-Star Game that marked the closing of Chicago Stadium, and then found that he still was adored by Chicago when he hoisted his retired jersey to the rafters of the new United Center.

Again, events conspired to alter Michael's career. With baseball embroiled in a strike, spring training in 1995 became a jumble. When Michael was asked to become a replacement player for the striking players on the White Sox major league roster, he quietly declined, not wishing to go against their union, mindful no doubt that he had been a member of the NBA Players Association.

With no end to the strike in sight, and his baseball career on hold, Jordan turned back to the NBA.

"I'm back," the announcement said after he had worked out with the Bulls for a week and then rejoined the team. "Eventually I just decided that I loved the game too much to stay away," he said. He also alluded to the fact that he was looking for new challenges, and that he'd like to teach the younger stars the respect he had learned for the league.

The Jordan effect was immediate, though his supporting cast with the Bulls was far different from the one he had left. Gone were such key players as forward Horace Grant, the unsung power forward so instrumental in the Bulls' three championship titles; center Bill Cartwright; and guard John Paxson. Scottie Pippen, who had become the Bulls' go-to player, was still there, and European star Toni Kukoc had joined a hybrid lineup that featured a wave of players trying to do the job of many stars.

Jordan returned with 17 games remaining in the 1995 season, and the Bulls were 31-31 and battling for a playoff spot. He then led his team in scoring in 12 of the 17 games, and the Bulls coasted into the playoffs.

Jordan was even more scrutinized in his comeback than he had been in spring training the previous year. Though he had only a week of practice before playing his first game in Indiana against the Pacers, expectations were unreasonably high. The Bulls lost to the Pacers in overtime and Jordan grimaced at his performance — 43 minutes; 19 points on some admittedly ragged shooting; 6 rebounds; 6 assists; and 3

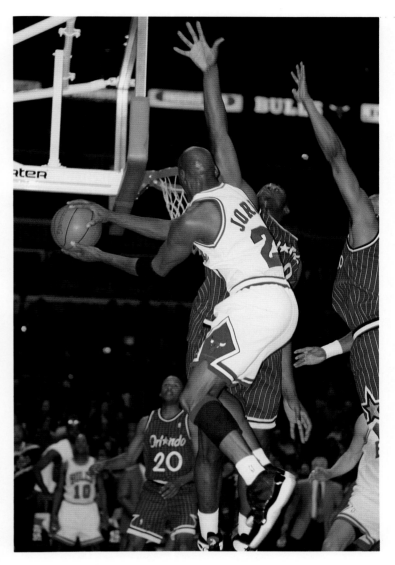

steals. "I certainly didn't want to go through this type of game at home," he said later.

There also was another difference — his jersey number was now 45, the same as he had worn at Birmingham. His number 23 hung in the rafters of the United Center, and he had said that it would stay there, because it was the last number his father had seen him wear. That resolve lasted until after the first game of the playoff series against Orlando, when the Magic's Nick Anderson said that Michael "didn't seem to be like the old Number 23 coming at you." In the next game, Jordan adopted his old jersey number and scored 38 points, though the jersey switch cost him a $5,000 fine from the NBA.

Jordan had a 48-point performance against Charlotte as the Bulls eliminated the Hornets in the first round of the playoffs series before they were eliminated by the Orlando Magic in six games. While some said he still showed the lingering signs of his layoff — not unusual — he nonetheless was the dominant player in both series. He averaged more than 30 points in nine playoff games, and in the game in which Chicago was eliminated from the playoffs he played himself into exhaustion trying to pull out a win.

Afterward, Jordan assured everyone that he would continue his NBA career with the Bulls, adding in typical Jordan fashion, "If they still want me."

The loss to Orlando in the 1995 playoffs, though a bitter pill for Jordan, was in fact a belssing of sorts because it triggered in him a drive to become the game's preeminent player once again. He had proven to himself, however painfully, that he simply couldn't walk back into the NBA and dominate the sport. Thus, the one factor that has always propelled him to the top – a challenge – became the motivating force that drove him to spend the off-season refashioning and retooling his game, much like a master craftsman takes a tarnished keepsake and restores it to its original luster.

Michael's brief sojourn into baseball was an extremely valuable learning experience for him. It offered a different set of challenges and a change of scenery that he believed he needed at that point in his life. It also gave him time to reflect on his accomplishments in the NBA and what the game really meant to him. This in turn established a platform within his psyche from which he would operate once he returned.

Michael also became more mellow in his approach to the game. Being away for most of two seasons, and then unexpectedly losing in the playoffs, made him realize just how much the game itself meant to him. All of the on-court pyrotechnics that had fueled his game and had helped bring him so much fame and wealth had become a part of his past. Now he could play and enjoy the game for its own sake, and concentrate on blending his still-awesome physical and competitive skills to achieve a different, yet deeper satisfaction from his achievements.

"I really am enjoying being a better all-around player," Jordan said while accepting his fourth MVP trophy just after the Bulls had beaten Orlando in four straight games for the 1996 Eastern Conference championship. That loss not only had eaten at Jordan throughout a record-setting 72-victory season, but it had also driven

Opposite: *Jordan and Dennis Rodman may have little in common in their lifestyles, but Michael usually had no problems with Rodman's play on the court. Rodman's great rebounding and defensive skills were key to the Bulls and Jordan winning three more NBA titles, from 1996 to 1998.*

Right: *When Jordan returned to the Bulls after playing baseball, he became a more complete player. His defensive skills never slackened, and he learned to use more of the court for his still-outstanding offense rather than relying so much on his slashing, driving style to get to the basket. Here he is seen shooting over the Knicks' Derek Harper in May 1996.*

him to his renewed push for excellence, which in turn brought a new and wider horizon to his game.

"I enjoy doing whatever it takes to win, even if it means guarding an opposing point guard, which is something I never did before," he said. "Or taking a step backward from my own game and letting Scottie [Pippen] grow as a player.

"But it's more than that. This trophy is more meaningful than the first three. I believe I am more appreciated as a complete player and I also have a better understanding of the game. I learned that no matter how great I was perceived as before I left, I couldn't simply come back and turn it on again. The game demands more than that, and I owed it to the game to meet those demands."

Teammate Steve Kerr looked at Jordan cradling his MVP trophy and marveled at what he had accomplished in a year's time. "He went back into the gym just a few days after we lost to Orlando, and that said something about Michael Jordan the person and the

player," Kerr said. "He started his quest with just one thing in mind – to get himself and his team back to the NBA Finals, and doing what he could to make his team better than the Orlando Magic which had beaten him a year ago. Mission accomplished."

Jordan also faced changes within the Bulls team itself, the most significant of which was the addition of forward Dennis Rodman. Rodman had been a very workmanlike player for the Detroit Pistons' two NBA championship teams a few years before he joined the Bulls, seemingly content to become the NBA's best rebounder as his contribution to a winning effort. But

he soon wore out his welcome at both Detroit, and then San Antonio, with his bizarre and unpredictable behavior on and off the court. His appearance was representative of his in-your-face attitude: he had scrolled his entire body with a variety of tattoos, sported various multi-colored hairstyles, and appeared in public in unconventional clothing such as dresses and wild hats. And while he continued to dominate the league's rebounders, no one was ever certain just what his intentions were.

Jordan had never played with anyone like Rodman, and despite Dennis's solid work under the boards

Opposite: *The Seattle Supersonics, particularly their star guard Gary Payton, did plenty of trash-talking before they played Jordan and the Bulls in the 1996 NBA Finals. It turned out to be a terrible mistake. Jordan demanded to be allowed to guard Payton and then destroyed him as the Bulls sent the Sonics packing in six games. Jordan was named MVP of the Finals.*

Right: *Although the Bulls had won a record 72 games in 1996, no one seemed ready to give them their due. Michael took care of that when they routed Seattle and their great forward Shawn Kemp in the 1996 NBA Finals. In the third game, Chicago was ahead 45-31 when Jordan took over and scored his team's next 15 points en route to giving the Bulls an insurmountable 3-0 series lead.*

Left: *Jordan's scoring touch never wavered after he returned to the Bulls in 1995 – he continued to average 32 points per game, the best in NBA history.*

Opposite: *With his first seven points in this December 1997 game, Jordan became the third-highest scorer in NBA history, with 27,409 points.*

which was a huge factor in the Bulls' continued championship success, many wondered just how the two stars could co-exist. There was little doubt that Michael ruled his locker room, and his teammates, including Rodman, accepted that he was the team's leader. That the Bulls continued to win, and somehow absorbed Rodman's manic and sometimes team-debilitating behavior, proved that Jordan was in control and that he accepted, up to a point, the distractions that accompanied Rodman's talents.

"We never tried to crowd Dennis. I never tried to change Dennis and I never let him change me," Jordan explained after the two helped Chicago win the 1996 NBA title. "When we stepped on the court, we had to have similar interests – to try and win a championship. It's been a very sensitive situation with Dennis, dealing with him and the personality I have and the attitude I bring to the game. . . . I think Dennis respected that. I never felt there was a chance that Dennis was going to cost us a chance to get back to the finals."

After the Bulls won their fifth title in 1997, Jordan acknowledged that Rodman was a major asset to the team's success. "Sure, he's going to go whacko every now and then, but we've come to live with that," Michael said. "I don't have a problem with Dennis . . . for all the different colors he may wear in his hair, or dresses, or whatever."

Rodman's antics made great media hype, but inevitably Jordan became the story. It wasn't too long into the 1996 season before fans everywhere had all but forgotten that Jordan had left the game for most of two seasons. It seemed almost as if he never had been gone as he led the Bulls to their record-setting season in 1996, followed by a 69-win season in 1997 and an NBA-tying best of 62 in 1998. He continued to win NBA scoring titles and barely missed a league MVP in 1997, which went to Utah's Karl Malone. He was again

an automatic selection for both the All-NBA first team and its all-defensive team.

Jordan capped his first full comeback season by helping the Bulls to a six-game victory over Seattle in the NBA Finals. That series was almost anti-climactic in an emotional sense to the four-game "revenge" sweep that Jordan had orchestrated over Orlando in the conference finals. In the second game, Chicago trailed by 18 points in the second quarter, but Michael scored 17 of his 25 second-half points in the third quarter to lead a second-half comeback. In the clinching fourth game, though suffering from a stomach flu, he bombed the Magic with 45 points – 16 in the fourth quarter – in a 106-101 victory, causing teammate Scottie Pippen to comment afterward:

"Judging by the look in Michael's eyes, we could have ridden him all day. I know I rode him. We all did. What's new?"

The Bulls won their fifth title in seven years against the Utah Jazz in 1997. Jordan's jump shot in the final seconds won the first game, and he set up Steve Kerr for the winning basket in the final seconds of the sixth game that clinched the championship. He averaged more than 32 points in the series, and 31 in the play-offs, and earned his fifth Finals MVP award. But even more than these stunning achievements, Michael will forever be remembered for what arguably was his single greatest performance, and certainly his most heroic, in the fifth game of the series. He had been racked for more than 18 hours by a stomach virus that didn't allow him to eat, leaving him weak and his legs feeling like rubber. Despite his illness, he came at the Jazz with a vengeance that was so amazing that several of them said afterward that they didn't even know he was sick. But he was so debilitated that he nearly fainted in the third quarter, and late in the game he had to lean on Pippen for physical support to get off the floor.

Left: *The Utah Jazz battled Jordan and the Bulls for NBA titles in both 1997 and 1998. Utah was led by two of Jordan's Olympic Dream Team teammates, Karl Malone (seen here with Jordan) and John Stockton, but neither was a match for Jordan and the Bulls.*

Opposite bottom: *Jordan celebrates the Bull's second "three-peat" in eight years with coach Phil Jackson. Jordan holds his MVP award, and Jackson raises the championship trophy.*

Yet he scored 38 points, including 15 in the fourth quarter, the last three being a decisive three-pointer with 25 seconds to play.

Bulls owner Jerry Reinsdorf marveled at the man for whom he was paying a record $30.6 million salary for his season's work. "The most courageous performance I have ever seen . . . the man could hardly walk, he could hardly breathe," Reinsdorf said afterward. "And he elevated himself to the point where he would not allow this team to lose.

Jordan did the same again during the 1998 season, when he had to carry a good deal of the team's burden while Pippen recovered from foot surgery for nearly half the season. As a team, the Bulls were not quite the juggernaut of previous seasons, but still finished with the second-best record in the league because Jordan didn't waver. He won his fifth NBA MVP award and his third straight scoring title. He was an automatic selection to the team's All-Star team and just as importantly to him, to its All-Defensive team.

Jordan also had to cope with the constant questions about his future. Team vice president Jerry Krause had indicated that it was time to tear apart the Bulls and begin rebuilding the team before it got old and tired. There was continuous speculation about the future of both coach Phil Jackson, who had termed the 1998 season "the last dance," and Pippen, and thus by extension, of Jordan himself. Jordan had said he would play only if Jackson were his coach and Pippen were a teammate.

As usual, Jordan blotted out all of this and performed brilliantly in leading the Bulls to their sixth NBA title of the decade, the second best performance by a franchise in NBA history (the Celtics of the sixties won nine). What helped was the personal challenge he took on from those who said that his glory days were finished, and he once more was the dominant player in the playoffs. Averaging more than 30 points a game, he also became the NBA's all-time best playoff scorer.

Astounding the pundits who had predicted their demise, the Bulls zoomed to a 3-1 lead in the Finals against the Utah Jazz. To the Bulls' chagrin, they couldn't clinch the title before their own fans in Chicago, and the sixth game was played in Utah where, as usual, Jordan saved his most electrifying performance for the title-winning game.

With Pippen playing a very reduced roll in the game because of an injured back, Jordan almost single-handedly kept the Bulls apace of the Jazz. He had 16 of the Bulls' 26 fourth-quarter points en route to a 45-point performance. He scored Chicago's last eight points in the final two and a half minutes, but everything came down to the final 40 seconds after Utah's John Stockton gave the Jazz a three-point lead.

Jordan took the ball down the court and swooped along the baseline to score a layup with 37 seconds to play, cutting the deficit to a point. The Jazz worked the ball to Karl Malone near Chicago's basket but Rodman stymied Malone's move toward the basket. As The Mailman prepared to pass the ball, Jordan stopped guarding Jeff Hornacek, stripped Malone of the ball, picked it up and headed toward Utah's basket.

"The moment started to come, and once you get the moment, you see the court and you see what the defense wants to do," he recalled. "I saw that moment and I felt the time tick to where I felt I had it where I wanted it. I stopped, pulled up and had an easy jump shot."

He was dogged by Bryon Russell but put on a quick stop-and-step move that almost turned Russell around and caused him to lose his balance. Jordan then had a clear shot from 19 feet and punctuated the net-only winning score with just 5.8 seconds to play by extending his arm to cap one of the most dramatic moments of his career.

Before he was handed his sixth MVP trophy and cradled the Bulls' sixth NBA championship trophy following the 87-86 victory, Jordan strode about the court with six fingers upraised, signifying each of the NBA titles that he had helped to produce. That gesture told it all.

Bulls owner Jerry Reinsdorf put everything into perspective when he said,"There has never been anybody like Michael Jordan, and I doubt that there ever will be in my lifetime."

INDEX

PICTURE CREDITS

Allsport USA: A. Bello 61bottom; A. Bernstein 68; J. Daniel 60left, 66; B. Gossage 67; A. Lyons 64; D. Pensinger 65.
Ray Amati: 7, 28, 37right, 41top right, 45bottom left and right, 54.
AP/Wide World Photos: 34, 51.
Bruce Bennett Studios: M. DiGirolamo 55; B. Miller 36right.
The Charlotte Observer: 2; Davie Hinshaw: 16.
Malcolm Emmons: 10, 13, 14top, 15, 17, 18, 21, 36left.
Naismith Memorial Basketball Hall of Fame: 22left.
Reuters/Archive Photos: M. Blake 71; S. Ogrocki 69; S. Wilson 8, 70.
Ron Schramm: 39top.
Carl Sissac: 1, 6, 9both, 11, 12left, 19, 20, 24, 26, 27, 30, 31, 32, 33, 35both, 37left, 39bottom, 41top left and bottom, 42, 43, 44, 46, 47, 48, 49top left and bottom right, 50left, 52right, 61top, 63.
Brian Spurlock: 62.
UPI/Bettmann Newsphotos: 4-5all, 14bottom left and right, 22left, 23, 25, 29, 38, 40, 45top, 49top right, 49bottom left, 52left, 53, 56, 57, 58, 59, 60right.
The Wilmington Star News: 12right.